READY, SET, GO!

IGNITING AFRICAN-AMERICAN MEN FOR CHRIST

DR. WILLIAM J. LEE

ISBN 978-0-692-08750-3

Printed in the United States of America

In honor of James Lee Jr., my dad, who modeled humility, hard work, and spirituality. Thank you for teaching me about Christ and always being there for me!

Contents

Introduction

The question may be raised, "Why have Bible study guides geared specifically for African-American men?" Let me be clear: The principles found in these Bible studies can be applied to any man from any cultural or ethnic background. The Word of God is true for every man apart from one's ethnicity and culture. The Great Commission given by Christ in Matthew 28:19-20 is to lead all people to the saving power of Jesus Christ. Once those people are saved, they are to disciple (Matthew 4:17-22; Mark 1:1-14-20).

Yet, over the last decade and a half while pastoring several different churches in three Midwestern states, I began to notice a pattern. The far majority of the congregation were women. Not only did the women attend more faithfully, but they also made up the majority of the teachers, board members, and ministry volunteers to children. Whenever we called for volunteers to assist in the work of the church, the women faithfully gave of their time and resources. I praise God for our women, but where are the men?

I began to ask myself, "Where are the men in the church?" I looked at several local men's ministry programs and saw they were almost non-existent. I looked at our deacons' department and noticed that the men were few. I had to ask myself, "What are we doing as a church to intentionally and effectively draw and disciple men to Christ?" I knew that the men's lack of participation in the church ministry was not due to a lack of Black men in the general population or in my particular city. All I had to do was drive along any inner-city street to see numerous Black men lined up along the street corners.

The lack of Black male presence in my church became a key concern for me. Unless we address the lack of Black men in the church, it could mean collateral damage to familial relationships as well as ecclesiastical work in general.

As a child growing up in a traditional African-American Seventh-day Adventist Church, I was exposed to men who were hard working professionals who attended church services weekly, but I always questioned why the church did not have more African-American men attending.

What can we do to reach more men in general for Christ? What can we do specifically to reach Black men for Christ? Black men are strong, capable, intelligent, and destined for greatness. Black men should understand their roots in God and their roots on this earth. We are special. As a child, my dad would say, "Son, there's nothing more powerful than a Black man that knows the Lord for himself."

Brothers, are you ready to achieve your God-given greatness? Are you ready to be changed by Christ? It's time to be ignited by God so that you, your wife, children, church, career, and community can be transformed for God's glory! It's time to shake up the world! Ready, Set, Go! Be ignited.

Instructions

This Bible study guide may be used for personal study. However, a man will receive additional insights and gain a fuller understanding of the material by going through the study guide with another man or in a small group. A men's prayer meeting or Bible study is ideal. The following format is recommended for a group.

1. Before the group meeting, each man should do the following:
   - Begin in prayer.
   - Read through the written section in the beginning of the chapter to get a good idea of the chapter's theme.
   - Look up the Bible verses and write answers to the questions.

2. When the group meets, the men should do the following:
   - Discuss the written section in the beginning of the chapter.

- Take turns reading the questions and Bible verses out loud and stating answers.
- Allow time for comments, questions, or a brief discussion.
- As a group discuss the "Thinking and Growing Together Section."
- Individually write out the goal you want to achieve as a result of the lesson.

3. When the group finishes a chapter, one or two men should attempt to give a brief summary of the chapter, and one or two men should share their individual goals with the group.

CHAPTER 1
Becoming a Spiritual Brother

Ellen White in her book **Education** writes, "The greatest want of the world is the want of men—men who will not be bought or sold, men who in their inmost souls are true and honest, men who do not fear to call sin by its right name, men whose conscience is as true to duty as the needle to the pole, men who will stand for the right though the heavens fall" (2002, p. 57).

Studies suggest that 90% of African-American men believe in God (Kunjufu, 2006). However, a much smaller percentage of these men attend weekly church services. The typical Black congregation is around 75% female and 25% male in spite of the fact that according to the The Pew Forum (2008), people of African ancestry were most likely than other ethnic groups to be part of a formal religion, with 85% being Christians.

Discussion Note: Why do you think Ellen White would suggest the "greatest want of the world is men who will not be brought or sold…true and honest"? Is spirituality a problem for Black men?

1. According to Genesis 1:26, what position did God give mankind?

   _____

   _____

Note: So God created mankind in His own image, in the image of God created He him; male and female created He them.

Psalm 8:5 "For thou hast made him (*mankind*) <u>a little lower than the angels</u>, and hast crowned him (*man*) with <u>glory</u> and <u>honour.</u>"

2. God gave mankind "dominion!" He created man "a little lower than the angels," yet what happen that caused man to run from God? See Genesis 3:6 –10.

   _____

   _____

Note: One simple <u>choice</u> can affect the rest of your life.

<u>Three Important Choices that Affect Men the Most:</u>
- ☐ Accepting Jesus Christ as their Lord and personal Savior.
- ☐ Choosing which woman God wants them to marry.
- ☐ Choosing in which careers they will work.

Ever since Adam <u>submitted his will to sin,</u> man has been on the run from God. Read 1 Corinthians 10:12 and Proverbs 6:27 and discuss how the choices we make every day affect us and those around us like ripples on a pond.

_____

_____

3. How did Adam's sin affect his relationship with God, his wife, and himself? Isaiah 59:1-2 gives us a hint.

_____

_____

4. What is so amazing about God's love for man? Read 1 John 4:8-11.

_____

_____

5. How then do we get back to God? John 3:1-8, 2 Corinthians 5:17- 18

_____

_____

The far majority of the "Great Men" in the Bible had major character flaws! Yet, they were able to overcome their flaws once they submitted to the power of God! As you evaluate your life, be on guard against discouragement. God wants you be a godly man! We were created in the image of God. Yet Satan may be looking over your shoulder and whispering in your ear, "You'll never become that kind of man. You've blown it too badly. There's no hope for you. You'll never break out of your old sin pattern!" However, remember, "Greater is He that is in you than he that is the world" (1 John 4:4).

6. According to James 4:7-8, what must mankind do in order to resist temptation and grow into spiritual men? See also John 15:1-10.

_____

_____

According to James, Spiritual Men must…
1. Submit to God – to His will and authority.
2. Resist the devil – don't linger in temptation or sin.
3. Draw nigh to God – abide in God's will.
4. Cleanse our hearts – remove known sins.
5. Purify our hearts – be renewed in God daily.

"But such a character is not the result of accident; it is not due to special favors or endowments of Providence. A noble character is the result of self-discipline, of the subjection of the lower to the higher nature--the surrender of self for the service of love to God and man" (White, 2002, p.57).

Thinking and Growing Together

Why do some men grow rapidly in their Christian faith once they become believers, and why do others struggle, seemingly taking as many steps backward as forward?

Set a Goal

Write out one goal you'd like to achieve as a result of this study.

CHAPTER 2

Brothers Want to Be Great

In his book *Kingdom Man* (2012), Dr. Tony Evans says, "Men long to be great." According to Evans, "Not only do we long to be great, but we also desire to be recognized as great. While women fantasize about relationships, men fantasize about greatness. While women fantasize about cuddling, men fantasize about conquering. As men, we want to *do* something. We crave significance, influence, and impact. This desire for greatness shows up in the sports we play, the wilds we roam, or the movies we watch." As Black men, our history is a history of greatness.

Discussion Note: What is "greatness is the eyes of the world" and what is "greatness in the eyes of Jesus"?

1. According to Matthew 20:20 – 28, what did Jesus say about the disciples' desire for greatness?

    _____

    _____

Note: It's okay to want greatness, but greatness comes with a high price tag. When James and John, known as the Sons of Thunder, sought a place of honor in Christ's kingdom, the other ten disciples gave them a difficult time for expressing their desire for significance. However, Jesus never corrected the two men for what they wanted.

God Want You to Be Great:

2. God wants men to be great so much that in Genesis 18:17-18, God refers to Abraham as not only a great man but also a great nation. What was God's desire for Abraham? Read also Genesis 12:2.

    _____

    _____

The Strength of Meekness:

Meekness is not walking around with a sunken chest, head down, and doing everything you're asked to do by those within your sphere of influence. That is not meekness at all. This is, rather, the world's attempt to cage and emasculate a male. It is the enemy's strategy to castrate men's drive and sideline the starters on God's kingdom team.

3. Meekness simply means submitting your power to a higher Control – it means submitting yourself to God's kingdom rule. Read Numbers 12:3 and discuss what makes men meek yet strong.

_____

_____

The Lord's Charge to Joshua:

4. What are some key characteristics in man's quest to become great? Read Joshua 1:1-9. Pay special attention to verse 8.

_____

_____

Note: Men, what you never want to do in your desire to be great is to try to steal or usurp God's glory.

David's Greatness and Failure:

5. What did God tell David in 2 Samuel 7:9 as it relates to greatness?

_____

_____

Note: Keep in mind that this was God talking. God was the one telling Abraham and David that He planned to make their names great. God was going to see to it that their names were etched in stone.

Jesus and His Disciples Pursue Greatness:

6. How did Jesus define true greatness? Read Mark 10:33-34.

_____

_____

God stands in the locker room of our souls with a personal bid for greatness, as long as that greatness comes under His authority and is expressed in an effort to reflect His glory.

7. Can *ordinary* men achieve greatness in the sight of God? See John 14:12.

_____

_____

8. What does conversion have to do with greatness? Refer to Matthew 18:1-4.

_____

_____

Thinking and Growing Together

True greatness begins by aligning yourself with God's kingdom agenda to benefit others. You must first make the decision that not only do you want greatness, but that you are also going to pursue it according to God's methods.

Set a Goal

Write out one goal you'd like to achieve as a result of this study.

CHAPTER 3
Proud of Who I Am

Black men have historically suffered role conflicts. Slavery stripped Black men of their masculinity, forcing them to be submissive servants, useful solely because of their physical strength. Slavery's tragically negative impact is evident in the struggle of Black men to be respected as intelligent leaders and as wage-earners and supporters of their families (Bigby, 2003).

African males, before coming to the Americas, had a well-organized culture with distinctly defined masculine roles. The adult African male roles within family and culture were as husbands, providers, protectors, heads of the family, and leaders within the community (Franklin & Moss, 2011). When African males entered slavery, they were stripped of legal, civil, and human rights and forced to adopt dramatically different subhuman roles.

Discussion Question: As a Black man, how do you view yourself? Do you have natural self-esteem and self-worth? Do you feel stereotyped by society?

1. What two African countries are mentioned most often in the Bible? Read Genesis 2:13 and Psalms 105:23.

_____

_____

Note: Ethiopia is known in the Bible as Cush – Egypt is known as Mizraim.

2. Who inhabited the countries of Egypt and Ethiopia? Read Genesis 10:6.

_____

_____

Note: The continent of Africa was inhabited by two sons of Ham called Mizraim and Cush. *Mizraim* is translated Egypt and Cush as Ethiopia.

3. What does the Bible have to say about the Ethiopians? Read Jeremiah 46:9.

_____

_____

4. Name two popular Africans who were leaders in Israel. Read Exodus 2:10 and Numbers 27:18.

_____

_____

Note: The Nile is a river of the continent of Africa, and both Moses and Joshua were born to Israelite parents while Israel was enslaved in Egypt. Joshua was born of the tribe of Ephraim, which was of African descent, and Moses looked like an Egyptian (Exodus 2:15-19), which means both were Black men.

5. In what African country did Jesus spend his early years of life? Read Matthew 2:13, 14.

_____

_____

6. What would eventually happen to the Africans? Read Psalms 68:31.

_____

_____

7. What is God's plan for the Africans along with others who remain faithful to Him? Read Isaiah 11:11.

_____

_____

Note: The word *Cush* is translated as Ethiopia.

For further information about Blacks in the Bible, see http://www.blacksinthebible.net.

Thinking and Growing Together

How do you feel knowing that you can trace your African history back to the Bible? Do you have a sense of pride to know that your African descendants were kings and queens in the Bible? How do you feel today that in Jesus Christ you have value, worthy, and riches?

Set a Goal

Write out one goal you'd like to achieve as a result of this study.

CHAPTER 4

Sabbath Roots and the African Connection

Black Africans have a unique proclivity toward accepting the seventh-day Sabbath. Historically, Ethiopia and many other parts of Black Africa have been bastions of Sabbatarianism. Their isolation for centuries from the corrupting influence of Rome has allowed Africans to maintain much spiritual independence. Today, Christianity in general, and Sabbath-keeping in particular, is exploding in sub-Saharan Africa.

Ethiopia is a nation defined throughout its existence by its fidelity to the seventh-day Sabbath. Today, the numbers of Sabbath-keepers are exploding in Nigeria, Ghana, Kenya, Gabon, Congo, and elsewhere. The Sabbath is thriving in Africa because the Sabbath roots of Africa run deep, both in Scripture and historical practice.

Discussion Question: Islam suggest that Christianity is the "White man's religion." What are your thoughts? Do you agree or disagree? Why?

1. Where was the Garden of Eden? Read Genesis 2:10-13.

_____

_____

Note: "And the Lord God planted a garden eastward in Eden; and there he put the man whom he had formed" (Genesis 2:8). Then the majestic words become quite specific: "And a river went out of Eden to water the garden; and from thence it was parted, and became into four heads. The name of the first is Pison: that is it which compasseth the whole land of Havilah, where there is gold; And the gold of that land is good: there is bdellium and the onyx stone. And the name of the second river is Gihon: the same is it that compasseth the whole land of Ethiopia. And the name of the third river is Hiddekel [Tigris]: that is it which goeth toward the east of Assyria. And the fourth river is Euphrates" (Genesis 2:10-14). We know by basic geography that these rivers are in Africa.

2. Where and when did God create the Sabbath day? Read Genesis 2:1-2.

_____

_____

Note: Sabbath keeping began before sin on the continent of Africa and later spread to the rest of the world. Thus the people of African descent should be Sabbath-keepers. Sunday keeping is a European institution. Which day is the Sabbath? Read Genesis 2:1-4 and Exodus 20:10.

_____

_____

3. Which day comes immediately after the Sabbath? Read Matthew 28:1.

_____

_____

Note: All Christianity agrees that Jesus rose from the dead "early Sunday morning up upon the first day of the week."

4. On what grounds were the Hebrews commanded to keep the Sabbath? Read Deuteronomy 5:15.

_____

_____

Note: While slaves the Hebrews could not keep God's Sabbath, but now are freed, they are commanded to keep it as a sign of liberation from slavery. The people of African descent, also freed from slavery, should keep God's Sabbath for the same reason.

5. On what day did Jesus go to Church? Read Luke 4:16.

_____

_____

6. What day did Jesus say He was the Lord of? Read Matthew 12:8.

_____

_____

Additional scriptures about the seventh day Sabbath:

1. **Exodus 31:13** – "Speak thou also unto the children of Israel, saying, Verily my sabbaths ye shall keep: for it is a sign between me and you throughout your generations; that ye may know that I am the LORD that doth sanctify you."

2. **Isaiah 58:13 - 14** " If thou turn away thy foot from the sabbath, from doing thy pleasure on my holy day; and call the sabbath a delight, the holy of the Lord, honourable; and shalt honour him, not doing thine own ways, nor finding thine own pleasure, nor speaking thine own words: 14 Then shalt thou delight thyself in the Lord; and I will cause thee to ride upon the high places of the earth, and feed thee with the heritage of Jacob thy father: for the mouth of the Lord hath spoken it.

3. **Mark 2:27, 28** – "And he said unto them, The sabbath was made for man, and not man for the sabbath: Therefore the Son of man is Lord also of the sabbath."

4. **Hebrews 4:8, 9** – "For if Joshua had given them rest, God would not have spoken later about another day. There remains, then, a Sabbath-rest for the people of God."

Thinking and Growing Together

Did you know that God still commands the keeping of His original Sabbath day holy? Would you like to begin keeping the Sabbath holy?

Set a Goal

Write out one goal you'd like to achieve as a result of this study.

CHAPTER 5

Strongholds Imprisoning African-American Men

A stronghold is a forceful stubborn argument, rationale, opinion, idea, and/or philosophy that is formed and resistant to the knowledge of Jesus Christ. The skillful use of spiritual weapons in spiritual warfare is required to break a stronghold.

> "For though we walk in the flesh, we do not war after the flesh: 4 For the weapons of our warfare are not carnal, but mighty through God to the pulling down of strong holds; 5 Casting down imaginations, and every high thing that exalteth itself against the knowledge of God, and bringing into captivity every thought to the obedience of Christ (2 Corinthians 10:3-5).

Discussion Question: Have you seen the effects of strongholds in your life or in the lives of other African-American men? Discuss the strongholds you have seen in the lives of men.

1. What does Paul mean when he says in 2 Corinthians 10:4 that the "weapons of our warfare are not carnal, but mighty through God to the pulling down of strongholds"?

_____

_____

Ways Strongholds Affect Us

2. **The Fear of Intimacy** – Many African-American women complain about the Black man's lack of affection and attention. Whether or not this is true may be debated, but the perception is there. How can God positively affect this notion in our lives? Read 1 John 4:18.

_____

_____

3. **Fatherlessness** – There are some African-American men who are sometimes absent from the home. What does the Bible say about fathers and their children? Read Psalms 127:3, 5 and Malachi 4:5, 6.

_____

_____

4. **Fear of rejection** – No one likes to be rejected. Yet as African-American men, we are often rejected because of prejudice, racism, and discrimination. How can we deal with rejection from the bible? Read John 6:37 and Matthew 11:28-30.

_____

_____

The Warrior Mentality

5. When one has a warrior mentality, this stronghold has anger as its foundation. Read Genesis 10:8-9 and name the Black man named there that had this stronghold.

_____

_____

Note: A warrior mentality can result in higher rates of violence and homicide. Homicide is the leading cause of death for African-American males 15-34 years old.

6. Since strongholds are resistant and formidable, what special spiritual weapons can bring them down? Read Ephesians 6:17 and Hebrews 4:12.

_____

_____

7. What other spiritual weapons can we use to bring down strongholds? Read James 5:16 and Ephesians 6:13-17.

_____

_____

Our weapons are mighty and include the following:

W – Word of God (Eph. 6:17; Heb. 4:12)

E – Effective Prayer (James 5:16)

A – Armor of God (Eph. 6:13-17)

P – Praises of God (2 Chron. 20:21-23)

O – Offerings of God (Mal. 3:8-11)

N – Name of God (Prov. 18:10)

S – Spirit of God (Zech. 4:6)

Thinking and Growing Together

What stronghold you may have faced in the past or are facing right now, God is able to give you complete victory. Read Mark 5:1-20 and discuss how this demon-possessed man was able to find freedom in Jesus.

Set a Goal

Write out one goal you'd like to achieve as a result of this study.

CHAPTER 6

Marriage Is Hard Work for a Brother

Today, marriage and family are regularly viewed as social conventions that can be entered into and severed by the marital partners at will. As long as a given marriage relationship meets the needs of both individuals involved and is considered advantageous by both sides, the marriage is worth sustaining. If one or both partners decide that they would be better off by breaking up the marriage and entering into a new, better marital union, nothing can legitimately keep them from pursuing their self-interest, self-realization, and self-fulfillment. By contrast, the Bible makes clear that, at the root, marriage and family are not human conventions based merely on a temporary consensus and time-honored tradition. Instead, Scripture teaches that family was God's idea and that marriage is a divine, not merely human, institution. As African-American men, we must be willing to invest 100% of ourselves into the marriage relationship.

Discussion Question: Do you see marriage as hard work? What would it take to improve your marriage?

1. What is marriage and who established it? Read Genesis 2:18 – 25. Why did God establish marriage?

_____

_____

Note: Marriage is a covenant, a sacred bond between a man and a woman instituted by and publicly entered into before God and normally consummated by sexual intercourse. God's plan for the marriage covenant involves at least the following five vital principles:

2. *The permanence of marriage:* Marriage is intended to be permanent, since it was established by God (Matthew 19:6; Mark 10:9). Marriage represents a serious commitment that should not be entered into lightly or unadvisedly. It involves a solemn promise or pledge, not merely to one's marriage partner, but before God.

_____

_____

3. *The sacredness of marriage*: Marriage is sacred not just merely a human agreement between two consenting individuals (a "civil union"); it is a relationship before and under God (Genesis 2:22). Hence, a "same-sex marriage" is an oxymoron, a contradiction in terms. Since Scripture universally condemns homosexual relationships, God will never sanction a marital bond between two members of the same sex.

_____

_____

4. **The intimacy of marriage**: Marriage is the most intimate of all human relationships, uniting a man and a woman in a "one-flesh" union (Genesis 2:23 -25). Marriage involves "leaving" one's family of origin and "being united" to one's spouse, which signifies the establishment of a new family unit distinct from the two originating families.

_____

_____

5. **The mutuality of marriage**: Marriage is a relationship of mutual respect and love to another (Ephesians 5:25-30). The marriage partners are to be first and foremost concerned about the wellbeing of the other person and to be committed

DR. WILLIAM J. LEE

to each other in steadfast love and devotion. This involves the need for forgiveness and restoration of the relationship in the case of sin.

---

6. **The exclusiveness of marriage**: Marriage is not only permanent, sacred, intimate, and mutual; it is also holy (Genesis 2:22-25; 1 Corinthians 7:2-5). This means that no other human relationship must interfere with the marriage commitment between husband and wife. For this reason, Jesus treated sexual immorality of a married person, including even a husband's lustful thoughts, with utmost seriousness (Matthew 5:28; 19:9). For the same reason, premarital sex is also illegitimate, since it violates the exclusive claims of one's future spouse.

Extramarital "affairs" take many different forms:

- ☐ Activities affair
- ☐ Materialism affair
- ☐ Career affair
- ☐ Family affair
- ☐ Fantasy affair (which can include pornography)
- ☐ Love affair

7. How God does help us as men to love him unconditionally? Read Galatians 5:22-23.

_____

_____

Thinking and Growing Together

Since the goal of marriage is oneness, how can I achieve this goal physically, mentally, and spiritually in my marriage?

Set a Goal

Write out one goal you'd like to achieve as a result of this study.

CHAPTER 7

Moral Purity, Help a Brother Out

Let's be completely honest. Most men, married or single, face sexual temptation. No one can avoid completely the twenty-first century sensuous messages that emanate from magazine covers, movie ads, and television commercials. Add to this the multitude of sensuously dressed women and female exhibitionists who permeate our culture, and it's not difficult to understand why man "is drawn away by their own lust" (James 1:14) and tempted every day of their lives.

Discussion Question: As a Black man, what is the first thought that comes to your mind when you hear the phrase "moral purity"?

1. What did Jesus say about lust and sexually temptation? Read Matthew 5:27, 28.

_____

_____

2. What does Jesus mean when he says that the "light of the body is the eye," and how does that relate to moral purity? Read Matthew 6:22-23.

_____

_____

3. What did Job say he did with his eyes? Read Job 31:1 (NIV).

_____

_____

Note: To be tempted is not a sin. Temptation, however, can quickly lead to sin. Any man who deliberately enjoys and pursues an illegitimate sexual relationship with a woman in his mind has, in God's sight, already committed an immoral act. This kind of fantasy world is off limits for a man who desires to follow God fully.

4. Read Proverbs 5. List the consequences of moral failure described in the chapter.

    _____

    _____

5. Read Proverbs 7. List the consequences of moral infidelity described in the chapter.

    _____

    _____

6. What forms of temptation do you have to fight the most?

    _____

    _____

Does the following confession accurately describe you?
- ☐ I am a man.
- ☐ I am only a man.
- ☐ I am a man just like every man.
- ☐ I am a sinful man.
- ☐ I am a weak man.
- ☐ I am a needy man.

☐ I need to be changed.

☐ I cannot change myself.

☐ I need You, God, to change me.

☐ I need Your help and the help of my brothers, too.

Don't complain, blame others, make excuses, and look for sympathy; look at God and yourself and get real. When do you struggle most with sexual temptation? How do you actively fight against sexual temptation? Be specific, because how you handle temptation may be just the thing your brother needs to hear.

7. Can Jesus free me from sexual sin? Read John 8:36, Luke 19:10, and Philippians 4:13.

_____

_____

Thinking and Growing Together

What are some specific things we can do to maintain moral purity? What has worked in each of our lives? What hasn't worked? What are some things we can do to begin to communicate with our wives? Why do some men have difficulty in maintaining moral purity?

Set a Goal

Write out one goal you'd like to achieve as a result of this study.

CHAPTER 8

Black Man, Handle Your Anger

It is impossible to live without getting angry. It's a natural, God-created emotion. This is why Paul wrote, "Be angry, and yet do not sin" (Ephesians 4:26). To deny this emotion in others and ourselves can lead to some serious psychological, spiritual, and even physical problems. Many Black men struggle with issues of anger. Anger can be caused by several factors such as unemployment, racism, discrimination, poor finances, and societal pressures; however, Jesus Christ, the perfect Son of God, demonstrated that it is possible to express anger without sinning all throughout His earthly ministry.

Discussion Question: What does the Bible mean when it says, "Be angry, yet do not sin?"

1. When does anger become sinful? Read Proverbs 15:18.

_____

_____

Note: We all know people who consistently "fly off the handle." They're quick-tempered, allowing angry feelings to get out of control.

2. What counsel do we find in the Book of James 1:19, 20 as it relates to anger?

_____

_____

Note: "Hurt people hurt people."

3. What happens if we allow anger to linger in our heart? Read Ephesians 4:25-32.

_____

_____

Note: When we allow anger to linger, it can eventually turn into bitterness. To allow misunderstandings to persist can lead to bitterness and increasingly aggressive actions.

4. As a man, what counsel does the Bible give when we do become angry? Read Proverbs 16:32.

_____

_____

Note: Psalms 37:8-9: "Refrain from anger and turn from wrath; do not fret--it leads only to evil. 9 For evil men will be cut off, but those who hope in the LORD will inherit the land."

5. What warning did Jesus give in Matthew 5:22 regarding anger?

_____

_____

6. Solomon gives profound counsel as it relates to friendship. What is his counsel in Proverbs 22:24?

_____

_____

7. What is the ultimate solution for handling anger? Read Ezekiel 36:25-28.

_____

_____

Three Steps to Handling Anger:

1. *Before letting anger erupt, remember that God works through trials.* Think about how God would have you handle the situation, so that when people see your true colors, they are beautiful and not something of which to be ashamed. Consider how He might be maturing you in your faith and pray for Him to work in you, through the challenge. *Read Philippians 4:19.*

2. *Remember that no matter how justified we feel in our anger, God is present.* No matter how hopeless a situation seems and no matter how or agitating, a situation

may be – God is always there to help us deal with our anger in the right way. **Read 1 Corinthians 10:13.**

3. *If you can't change the person or circumstance which has angered, change yourself.* Anyone can return evil for evil, but it takes a courageous man in Christ to allow love to flow from our hearts instead of hatred. Even if your mind wants to take revenge, talk to God about helping you have the willpower to offer forgiveness. It might not change the external problem, but it will change your internal ability to handle the situation. **Read 1 John 1:9; Psalms 51:1-10.**

Thinking and Growing Together

Do I tend to get angry quickly and frequently? Do I find that angry feelings persist and linger? Do I want to take matters into my own hands and get even with others who make me angry? What have you discovered is the best way to handle your anger?

Set a Goal

Write out one goal you'd like to achieve as a result of this study.

CHAPTER 9

Black Men Need a Good Reputation

When you hear the names President Barack Obama, Michael Jordan, Reverend Jesse Jackson, and Tiger Woods, what immediately comes to mind? A reputation is something that everyone has and cannot escape. Whether good or bad, reputation is something that sums up who we really are, whether or not we want it. We cannot buy reputation; we cannot deny it; we cannot inherit it; and we cannot change it without changing ourselves. Building a good reputation is important to being a godly man.

Discussion Question: Do I get positive feedback from those closest to me (my wife, my children, and my friends) that would indicate I have a good reputation?

1. What does the Bible say about reputation and should I be concerned as a man? Read Ecclesiastes 7:1.

_____

_____

Note: Reputation is not what we say we are. Basically, reputation is "Our lives are speaking so loudly about us that people cannot hear what we say about ourselves." Reputation is not what we think of ourselves, but rather how we are known to others. It is a predictable response to a future influence or situation.

2. What can spoil my good reputation? Read Ecclesiastes 10:1.

_____

_____

Note: A good reputation can be spoiled by a little folly. Ecclesiastes 10:1 states, "Dead flies cause the ointment of the apothecary to send forth a stinking savour: so doth a little folly him that is in reputation for wisdom and honour." It does not matter how good your reputation has been for how long, it can become a stink with a little folly.

3. What does the Bible say about a good name? Read Proverbs
   22:1.

_____

_____

Note: We do not have to protect a good name from those who
are loose with their tongue. They build their own reputation,
and no one believes them when they speak ill of those of good
reputation.

4. When you hear the names Cain, Job, and Rahab, what
   immediately comes to your mind?

_____

_____

Note: Reputation will follow us far beyond every victory we win
in life, and the sooner we change and build a good reputation,
the more lasting the good reputation will be.

5. What was one of the major qualifications of selecting deacons in Acts 6:1-8? Read again Acts 6:3.

_____

_____

6. How important is it to guard your tongue and heart as a man? Read James 3:5-15.

_____

_____

Note: "Your word is your bond."

7. What counsel does the Apostle Paul give us in Ephesians 4:25-32 that will help us as men guard our reputations?

_____

_____

Thinking and Growing Together

Are we aware of any attitudes and actions in our lives right now that are hurting our reputations? What steps can we take immediately to rebuild our reputations in those particular areas? What one thing would you like to do immediately to begin to enhance your reputation as a Christian man?

Set a Goal

Write out one goal you'd like to achieve as a result of this study.

CHAPTER 10

Black Men Spend Time with God

The devotional life has been called by many names: daily devotions, morning watch, quiet time, time with the Lord. The fact that Christians can usually describe it, however, does not necessarily mean that many of them practice it. Actually, few believers meet daily with the Lord on a consistent basis. As Black men, we are often times overloaded with trying to balance work, family, and life. It is critical that we have a specific daily time when God speaks to us through His Word, and the believer responds in prayer.

Discussion Question: As a man, do you ever find yourself too tired to spend quality time with God?

1. The scriptures give us many examples of Bible characters who had daily devotions. After the following passages, write down the name of the man, what he did or desired regarding his fellowship with God, and in your opinion, why this was true.

☐ Read Genesis 19:27.

_____

_____

☐ Read Psalm 63:1-2.

_____

_____

☐ Read Psalm 27:4.

_____

_____

☐ Read Exodus 33:14-15.

_____

_____

☐ Read Mark 1:35.

_____

_____

☐ Read Philippians 3:10.

_____

_____

2. How was the king to read the scriptures, according to Deuteronomy 17:18-20?

_____

_____

3. When should we pray? Read Luke 18:1.

_____

_____

4. What does 1 Thessalonians 5:17 say?

_____

_____

5. What can be some hindrances to prayer? Read Psalms 66:18 and Isaiah 59:2.

_____

_____

6. What does James 5:13-18 tell us about the power of prayer?

_____

_____

7. When Peter was in prison, what did the church do for him? Read Acts 12:5.

_____

_____

Thinking and Growing Together

When have you found the best time is for you to pray?
What answers have you seen to prayer? What has been
your experience when you did not have a regular devotional time with God?

Set a Goal

Write out one goal you'd like to achieve as a result of this
study.

CHAPTER 11

Brothers Understand True Headship

The primary principle upon which your destiny forms as a man, both now and in the future, involves the concept of headship. The Apostle Paul introduced this truth into the setting of a chaotic Corinthian church located directly in the heart of the most licentious city of the first century. In Corinth, everything was out of order. In fact, it was a free-for-all, resulting in unprecedented amounts of divisions, pain, and confusion within the church. In this lesson we understand that headship isn't about essence or being; it is about function.

Discussion question: How do you understand the whole idea of the *head*?

1. The idea of headship includes covering, provision, protection, guidance, and responsibility. These characteristic define Christ's relationship with the church as the head of the church. In Ephesians 5:25-33, we read that a man is to emulate Christ in his marriage as head. How is this possible?

_____

_____

Note: Headship isn't about essence or being; it's about function. We know that Christ's ontological being is the same essence of God, but when it came to functioning on Earth, Jesus came under God to carry out the divine plan. Theology also clearly tells us that Jesus is equal to God. Headship doesn't determine or reflect a lack of equality.

2. How do you understand 1 Corinthians 11:3 where we read that "the man is the head of a woman?"

_____

_____

Ellen White:

"Neither husband nor wife is to make a plea for rulership" (*Testimonies for the Church*, p. 47).

"Woman should fill the position which God originally designed for her, as her husband's equal" (*Adventist Home*, p. 231).

"He should be very tender and gentle toward his wife, who is his equal in every respect" (*Adventist Home*, p. 227).

3. According to Genesis 2:24, when a man and woman are joined together, they become one flesh.

_____

_____

Note: Man and woman were created equal in the image of God (Genesis 1:26, 27).

The problem in marriages today isn't that we have too many women who don't want to submit. The problem is that we have too many men who don't want to submit to the headship of Christ.

4. Who is the head of the Church? Read Ephesians 5:23 and Colossians 1:18.

_____

_____

Our women, sisters, daughters and wives have been given to us by God, and each and every one of them is beautiful in His sight. Their fulfillment depends to some extent on us. They need mature men just as we need mature women. How many of us will decide to become real men? How many of us will admit that what we most need is to become godly men?

5. Read Genesis 2:23, 1 Timothy 5:8, 1 Peter 2:9. How do you understand the role of *head* in these verses?

_____

_____

6. As a man, how can I become a better leader in the home and community? Read Proverbs 3:5-6.

_____

_____

7. Jesus calls mankind to fully surrender to Him. How is this possible? Read John 15:1-5.

_____

_____

Thinking and Growing Together

If you find that you are out of alignment with God, you need to get back in it as quickly as possible through confession and repentance. 1 John 1:9 says, "If we confess our sins, he is faithful and just to forgive us *our* sins, and to cleanse us from all unrighteousness."

Set a Goal

Write out one goal you'd like to achieve as a result of this study.

CHAPTER 12

Brothers, Change the World

The path to a better life begins with you. It begins with a right choice. When you make the right decision to fully surrender your life to Christ, Jesus will work in you both His will and the fulfillment of His will in your life. You become a better man by aligning yourself under the comprehensive rule of God over every area of your life. What do you desire in life? Do you desire to be a God-fearing man? Do you desire to be a God-fearing husband? If you have children, what is your desire for them? Do you want to be a better father? Can you be a better you? The life you've always wanted is just before you! Let God change you, and then change the world!

Discussion Question: What are some of your biggest dreams and desires in life?

1. Most men have a desire to be "successful." (Success can mean different things to different people: Money, good name, respected, family together, occupation & work.) What you want, you have to work at. Read Proverbs 6:6-11.

_____

_____

Note: Those who are successful in life understand the necessity of hard work (i.e., athletes and businessmen).

2. How do we understand the words of Jesus in John 10:10 as they relate to the life you really desire?

_____

_____

3. Is it true that men desire *respect* as one of their top priorities/
    necessities?

    _____

    _____

Read Matthew 7:12 – "So in everything, do to others what you
would have them do to you, for this sums up the Law and the
Prophets."

4. If I desire a godly marriage, what part do I play as a man?
    Read Ephesians 5:25-29.

    _____

    _____

5. If I desire godly children, what part do I play as a man? Read
    Colossians 3:21.

    _____

    _____

Note: Proverbs 15:1 "A soft answer turneth away wrath: but grievous words stir up anger."

Adventist Home: Father's Position and Responsibilities, p. 213

> **Submit the Will to God.**--To the man who is a husband and a father, I would say, Be sure that a pure, holy atmosphere surrounds your soul. . . . You are to learn daily of Christ. Never, never are you to show a tyrant like spirit in the home. The man who does this is working in partnership with satanic agencies. Bring your will into submission to the will of God. **Do all in your power to make the life of your wife pleasant and happy**. Take the word of God as the mode of your counsel. In the home live out the teachings of the word.

Never become too busy for your wife! Make sure that she understands that you love her, not just in word, but in deed and action. Life can get busy very fast, but always make time for your family. God has placed two women in your life--treat them well!

6. Every Christian man should desire a relationship with God! Read Jeremiah 1:5, 29:11, and Matthew 6:33.

7. What is God's invitation to you as a man? Read Matthew 11:28-30.

8. Life begins as you begin to walk with the Lord Jesus Christ. What will Jesus do for me as I surrender myself to Him? Read 2 Corinthians 5:17.

9. As God changes my heart, mind, and spirit what must I now begin to do? Read Matthew 28:19, 20.

_____

_____

Note: Remember, you are your brother's keeper! Now change the world by the power of the Holy Spirit living in and through you. Ready, Set, Go! Be Ignited.

Thinking and Growing Together:

What are you doing about the things you really want in life? Are you ready to fully surrender to the rulership of Christ?

Set a Goal

Write out one goal you'd like to achieve as a result of this study.

If you would like more information on a personal relationship with God, please contact me at LeewjL@hotmail.com. If you enjoyed this Bible Study, please recommend it to your friends.

Thank you very much.

References

Anyike, J. (1994). *Historical Christianity African centered.* Chicago, IL: Popular Truth.

Arterburn, S., Stoeker, F., & Yorkeym, M. (2000). *Every man's battle.* Colorado Springs, CO: Water Brook Press.

Bigby, J. (2003). Care of Blacks and African Americans. In *Cross Cultural Medicine* (1st Ed., pp. 29-60). Philadelphia, PA: American College of Physicians.

Connor, M. E., & White, J. (2006). *Black fathers: An invisible presence in America.* Mahwah, NJ: Lawrence Erlbaum Associates.

Evans, T. (2012). *Kingdom man.* Nashville, TN: LifeWay.

Franklin, J. H., & Moss, A. A. (2011). *From slavery to freedom: A history of African Americans.* New York, NY: Alfred A. Knopf.

Kunjufu, J. (2006). *Adam! Where are you? Why most Black men don't go to church* (1st ed.). Chicago, IL: African American Images.

Macon, L. L. (1997). *Discipling the African-American male: How to get Black men into church and keep them there.* Nashville, TN: James C. Winston.

McCray, W. (1990). *The Black presence in the Bible.* Chicago, IL: Black Light Fellowship.

The Pew Forum. (2008, February). U.S. Religious Landscape Survey. Retrieved from http://religions.pewforum.org/pdf/report-religious-landscape-study-full.pdf

White, E. (2002). *Education.* Nampa, ID: Pacific Press.

White, E. (2002). *The Adventist Home.* Nampa, ID: Pacific Press.

White, E. (2002). *Testimonies for the Church, Volume 7.* Nampa, ID: Pacific Press.

About the Author

Pastor Dr. William J. Lee Sr., was born in Benton Harbor, Michigan to two Christian, Seventh-day Adventist parents, Mr. James Lee Jr, and Mrs. Jean Lee.

At an early age his parents instilled within him a strong desire to serve God and to love the church. He was baptized at the age of 11 years old and has faithfully remained in the church ever since.

Dr. William J. Lee is a gifted preacher of God's Word. He preaches a powerful message for this end-time generation. Flowing under a strong anointing, Pastor Lee is a trailblazer. His messages touch the hearts of adults and youth alike. He strongly believes that Jesus Christ is soon to return, thus he ministers with great passion and enthusiasm proclaiming the everlasting gospel of Jesus Christ.

Dr. Lee has served the Lake Region Conference for the past 16 years. He has Pastored the Trinity Temple SDA Church, in Kalamazoo, MI, the Jackson Summit church in Jackson, MI, Bethel SDA Church in Grand Rapids, MI, the Capitol City SDA Church in Indianapolis, Indiana, and currently serves as the Senior Pastor of the historic Shiloh Seventh-day Adventist Church in Chicago, IL.

Before his call to ministry, Pastor Lee spent 1 year at Tuskegee University majoring in Chemical Engineering. However in 1999, he felt to the call to ministry. Thus, he holds the Bachelor of Arts Degree in Religion from Oakwood University in Huntsville, Alabama; (Magna Cum Laude) the Master of Divinity Degree from Andrews University in Berrien Springs, Michigan; and he has earned the Doctor of Ministry Degree from Andrews University concentrating in Urban Ministries. His dissertation was entitled, "A strategy to increase African-American male membership in the Adventist Church."

Dr. Lee also serves as the Men's Ministry Director for the Lake Region Conference of Seventh-day Adventist.

He also currently serves as the host of a television show on 3ABN's Dare to Dream Network called, "For Guys Only" which can be seen weekly throughout the world.

Pastor Lee married his high school sweet-heart, Ms. Latoria Thomas- Lee. Latoria holds a Master of Education degree in Adult and Higher Education with a concentration in College Student Affairs Leadership from Grand Valley State University. She currently serves as the Director of Career Services for the School of Public Health at Indiana University-Purdue University in Indianapolis, IN.

The Lee's have two children William and Christopher.

Any success achieved by Pastor Lee, is always attributed to the hand of God, and to those people who have helped him along the way. One of his favorite Bible text is Romans 8:31, "What shall we then say to these things? If God *be* for us, who *can be* against us?"

He enjoys basketball, tennis, long walks with family, and Carnival cruises with his family.

NOTES

CPSIA information can be obtained
at www.ICGtesting.com
Printed in the USA
FFOW02n2043180418
46297907-47817FF